SIMPLE MACHINES

LEVERS

Nancy Dickmann

BROWN BEAR BOOKS

Published by Brown Bear Books Ltd
4877 N. Circulo Bujia
Tucson, AZ 85718
USA

and

Leroy House
436 Essex Rd
London N1 3QP
UK

ISBN 978-1-78121-398-8 (library bound)
ISBN 978-1-78121-428-2 (paperback)

Library of Congress Cataloging-in-Publication Data available on request

Text: Nancy Dickmann
Design Manager: Keith Davis
Picture Manger: Sophie Mortimer
Editorial Director: Lindsey Lowe
Children's Publisher: Anne O'Daly

Manufactured in the United States of America
CPSIA compliance information: Batch#AG/5608

Picture Credits
The photographs in this book are used by permission and through the courtesy of:

Front Cover: Shutterstock: inset, Avalon Studio main.
Interior: 123rf: budabar 14–15; Alamy: Agencja Fotograficzna Caro 18–19, Robert Harding 12–13; Dreamstime: 10; Getty Images: Ole Graf 4–5; istockphoto: cjp 6, Lise Gagne 21t, Frank Huang 18, Kall9 8–9, 20b, peepo 16–17, S Walls 6–7; Shutterstock: 4, Avalon Studio 20–21, Marc Dietrich 11, C. Jansuebsri 16, Razoomanet 13, Michael Rosskothen 12, zsolt_uveges 1, 20l; Thinkstock: istockphoto 10–11, 14, 21b.

All other artwork and photography © Brown Bear Books.

t-top, r-right, l-left, c-center, b-bottom

Brown Bear Books has made every attempt to contact the copyright holder. If you have any information please contact: licensing@brownbearbooks.co.uk

Websites
The website addresses in this book were valid at the time of going to press. However, it is possible that contents or addresses may change following publication of this book. No responsibility for any such changes can be accepted by the author or the publisher. Readers should be supervised when they access the Internet.

Words in **bold** appear in the Useful Words on page 23

Contents

What Is a Lever?

A lever is a long bar. It lies across a balance point. The balance point is the **fulcrum**. If you push one end of a lever down, the other end goes up. Levers can lift or move things.

WOW!

Scissors are a pair of levers. They work together. They push the blades through paper.

A seesaw is a lever.
The fulcrum is in the middle.
When you sit on one end,
the other goes up.

What Are Machines?

Levers are a type of **machine**.

Machines are all around us.

It takes **energy** to move or lift something.

Machines can make these jobs easier.

Tools are made of simple machines. A spade's handle is a lever. Its blade is a **wedge**.

A machine can be very simple.
It can have one or two parts.
To do more complicated jobs,
machines need more parts.
The parts work together.

Levers and Forces

A **force** is a push or a pull.
You push on a lever.
It increases the force of your push.
That makes lifting easier.

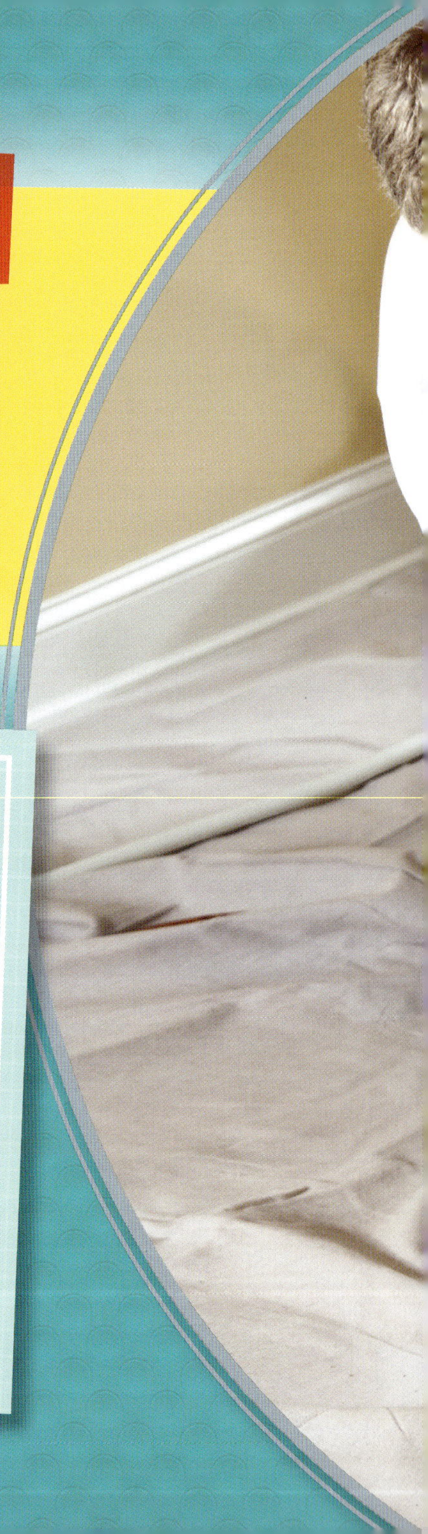

Forces

A lever can help lift a heavy **load**.

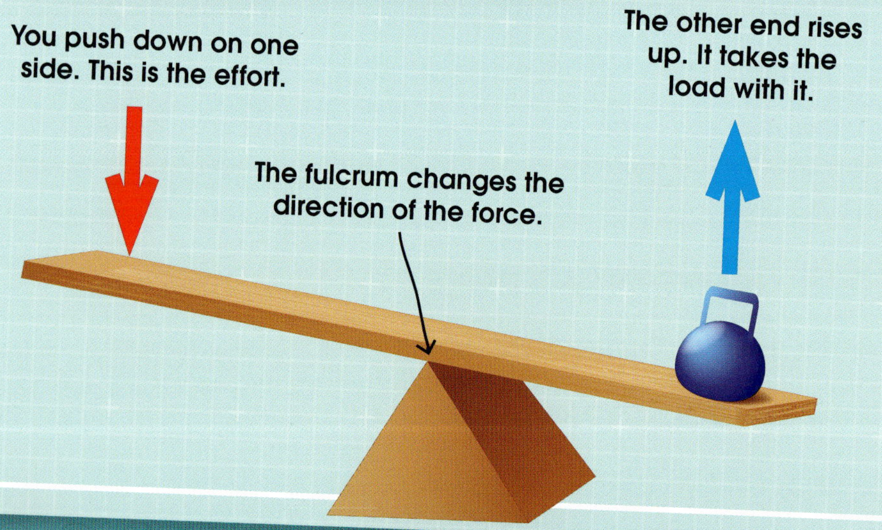

A lever can help lift the lid of a paint can. The lid is close to the **fulcrum**. The end you push on is much longer. Your **effort** is spread over a longer distance. This makes lifting easier.

Classes of Levers

There are three classes of levers. They have the same parts. The parts are arranged in different ways.

Class 1 lever

The **fulcrum** is in the middle. You apply **effort** on one end. The **load** is at the other end.

Class 2 lever

The fulcrum is at one end. You apply effort on the other end. The load is in the middle.

Class 3 lever

The fulcrum is at one end. The load is at the other end. You apply effort in the middle.

Levers in the Past

Levers are very simple machines. People have used them for thousands of years.

Ancient Greek ships used oars. The oars are levers. They help the boat travel faster.

WOW!

Balance scales were invented long ago. They weigh things. The **fulcrum** is in the middle.

Ancient Egyptians used a shaduf. A bucket hangs from one end. The bucket scoops up water. People still use a shaduf in some countries.

Types of Levers

We still use levers today. A hammer with a claw is a lever. It can pull a nail out of wood. A wheelbarrow is a lever. It helps us move heavy loads.

A fishing rod is a lever. The fish is the **load**. Raising the rod lifts the fish.

An excavator scoops up earth. It has a bucket on a long arm. The arm is a lever. It moves the bucket up and down.

Everyday Levers

Pliers have two levers. They work together. They join in the middle. You squeeze the handles. The other ends pinch together.

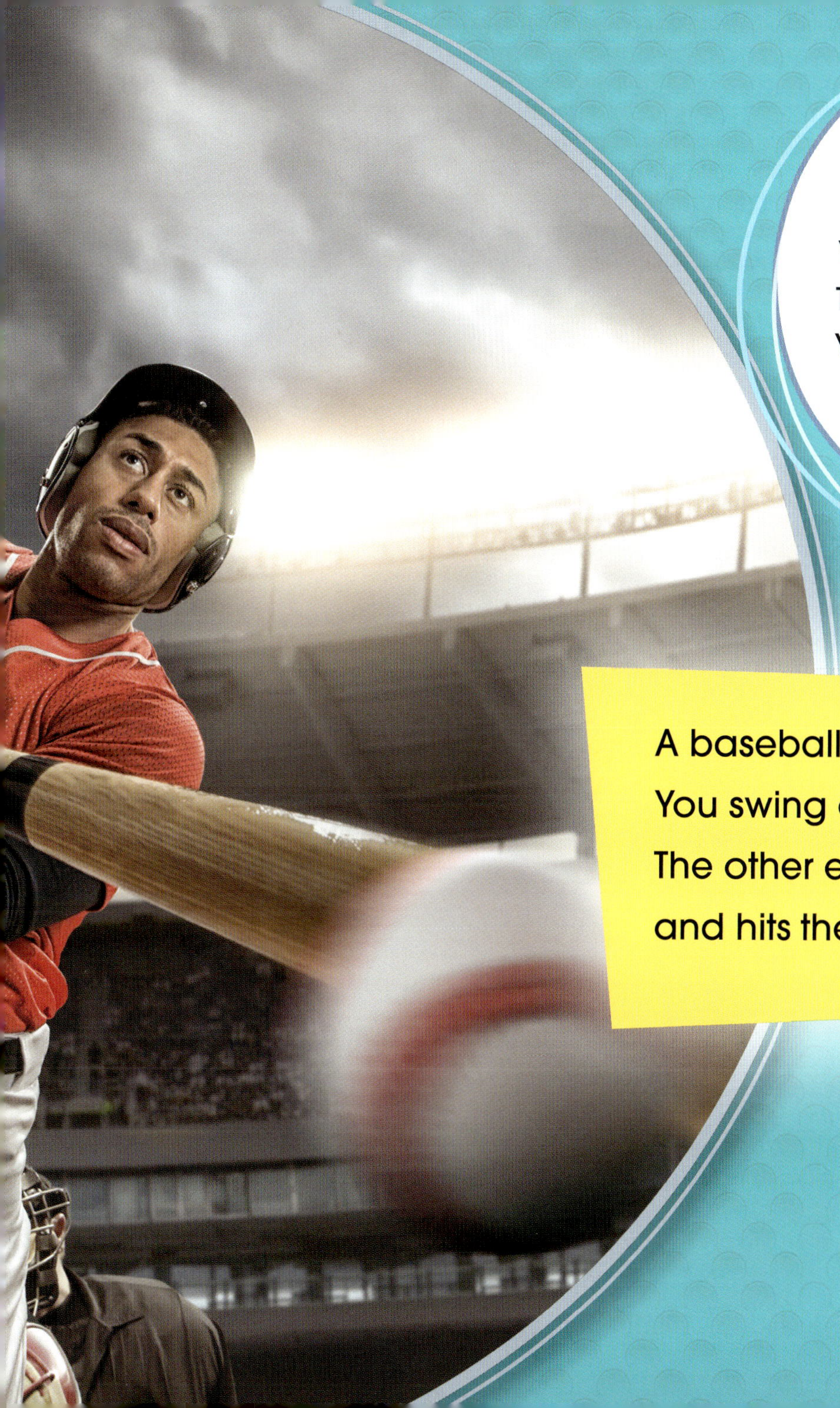

WOW!

Your arm can be a lever. The elbow is the **fulcrum**. Your muscles provide the **effort**. They make your forearm move.

A baseball bat is a lever. You swing one end of the bat. The other end moves faster and hits the ball.

Compound Machines

Levers are simple machines.

So are wedges and wheels.

Simple machines can work together.

They make **compound machines**.

The arm of a stapler is a lever. Pushing on it makes a staple come out. The staple's points are **wedges**. They push through paper.

A tow truck is a compound machine. It has wheels to roll along. It has a lever at the back. A **pulley** helps lift. These simple machines all work together.

Spot the Lever!

Can you find the levers in these pictures?

1

2

3

4

5

Try It!

Make your own lever.
Can you find the best place to put the fulcrum?

You will need:

- **ruler**
- **spool of thread**
- **a heavy book**
- **a friend to help you**

1. Lay the ruler across the spool of thread. The spool is the fulcrum. Put the book on one end of your lever. This is your load.

2. Push down on the other end to lift the book. How hard was it?

3. Move the spool farther from the book and try again.

4. Move the spool closer to the book and try again.

Which set-up made it easiest to lift the heavy book?

Useful Words

compound machine A machine that is made up of smaller machines. It can have several different simple machines.

effort The force that pushes on a lever.

energy The ability to do work. We use energy to lift or move things.

force A push or a pull.

fulcrum The point that a lever moves around.

load The object that a lever tries to move.

machine Something that helps us do work.

pulley A simple machine. It has a wheel with a rope running over it. Pulleys can help lift heavy objects.

wedge A simple machine with angled sides. Wedges can split things apart.

Answers to page 20–21: Did you spot the levers?**1.** The baseball bat; **2.** the screwdriver; **3.** the excavator's arm; **4.** the wheelbarrow (the wheel is the fulcrum); **5.** the fishing rod.

Find out More

Websites

www.britannica.com/technology/simple-machine

www.explainthatstuff.com/toolsmachines.html

www.msichicago.org/play/simplemachines/

Books

Levers
Sian Smith, Heinemann-Raintree 2012

Levers at Work
Dawn Lamachia, Enslow Publishing 2015

Levers in My Makerspace
Tim Miller, Crabtree Publishing Company 2017

Index